Pet Help

by Nancy Lollo

Glenview, Illinois • Boston, Massachusetts • Chandler, Arizona
Upper Saddle River, New Jersey

We help pets.

I help dogs.
I help dogs at dog school.

This dog will learn.
It will learn at dog school.

Sit, dog, sit.
Good dog.

I am a vet.

I help sick pets.

I like to help.